0802278

ALBERT
PUJOLS

I also dedicate this book to you, my readers, who I hope will enjoy reading it and, perhaps, learn a few lessons about the importance of dedication and hard work. I also hope you will realize, if you don't already, that neither talent nor fame equates to virtue, and that hitting and catching a ball can be great fun and very thrilling, but baseball is, after all, only a game. Most people don't have enough talent to play in the major leagues, but everyone has the capacity and, perhaps, the responsibility to use the talents that they do have to achieve their own best dreams and most important goals. Although the work may not pay as well, finding a cure for a disease, reversing global warming, and striving to make the world a more tolerant, just and peaceful place, may, in the end, be more long-lasting and more satisfying.

With great thanks and appreciation to everybody whose time and talents have contributed to this book, including Janie DeVos, John Douglas, and Joe Gannon, as well as to Gina Shaw, for her patience and good humor.

Chief Researcher: **Janie DeVos**
Copy Editor: **John Douglas**
Design and Layout: **Joe Gannon**

This book was not authorized by Albert Pujols or Major League Baseball.

Cover photo: Jim McIsaac/Getty Images

Copyright © 2007 by Richard J. Brenner/East End Publishing, Ltd.
All rights reserved. Published by Scholastic Inc., 557 Broadway, New York, NY 10012, by arrangement with East End Publishing, Ltd.
Printed in the U.S.A.

ISBN 978-0-545-03545-3

4   5   6   7   8   9   10   40   15 14 13 12 11 10 09 08 07

01/25/08
RR 6
$ 4.99

CONTENTS

ONE • Coming to America 5

TWO • The Crack of Thunder 10

THREE • The Sound of Cannons 17

FOUR • On a Fast Track to the Big Time 24

FIVE • Rookie of the Year 35

SIX • The Second Time Around 46

SEVEN • Hitting New Heights 56

EIGHT • A Step Away 65

NINE • A Most Valuable Player 77

TEN • Winning It All 86

Statistics 95

ONE

Coming to America

Jose Alberto Pujols was born January 16, 1980, in Santo Domingo, which is the capital city of the Dominican Republic. The DR, a Spanish-speaking country, occupies two-thirds of the island of Hispaniola, and sits amid the warm waters of the Caribbean, 670 miles southeast of Key West, Florida. The other third of the island is occupied by Haiti, whose inhabitants speak French.

In addition to the difference in languages between the two countries, baseball is little played or followed in Haiti, while in the DR baseball is played with great passion and is the nation's most popular sport. In fact, since 1956, when Ozzie Virgil became the first Dominican to break into the major leagues, the DR, with a population of only nine million people, has sent more than 400 players to the big leagues, far more than any other country in the world, except for the United States.

The river of talent flowing north has not only been about quantity, but also about quality, with the DR contributing a constant flow of future All-Stars to the majors, including current superstars such as Vladimir Guerrero, David Ortiz, Jose Reyes, and Miguel Tejada.

Albert began playing baseball when he was eight years old, and quickly started to dream of becoming one of those players who would follow the Gulf Stream from the DR to the big leagues. He received his first coaching from his father, Bienvenido,

"I don't compare myself to other players. I just want to be Albert Pujols. I don't want to compare myself with anyone else."

who was a well-regarded, if not-quite-major-league-caliber pitcher in the DR. Because his father was often away, and his mother didn't remain with the family for long, Albert was mostly raised by his grandmother, whose name is America, and his uncle, Antonio Joaquin dos Santos, who was one of America's eleven children.

Like many of the Dominican players before him, Albert grew up in dire poverty and early on had to use a stick for a bat and limes, which are plentiful in the DR, as balls. And, while most children in the United States take owning a fielding glove for granted, Albert's first mitt was a milk carton that was cut out to resemble the shape of a glove.

Although he didn't grow up with the benefit of having his parents as a constant presence in his life, Albert didn't lack for attention or affection from the large extended family with which he lived. In fact, it was his uncle Antonio who supplied young Albert with most of the baseball equipment that he did receive, and in whose house he lived for seven years.

"My family did whatever they could to help me get a pair of spikes or batting gloves," recalled Albert. "It's because of their support that I was able to make it to the big leagues."

"I can't believe my uncle Antonio died, that he's no longer here. I still close my eyes and see his face."

While Albert loved to play baseball, he didn't show any great promise in his early years of playing the game. In fact, when he was 16 years old, the age when major league teams are allowed to sign the DR's top prospects, Albert didn't draw any interest at all.

In the summer of 1996, a few months after Albert's failure to catch the eye of major league scouts, he moved to the United States with his father and grandmother, following in the footsteps of millions of immigrants who have come to the U.S. in hope of building a better life. The family first settled in New York City, which has a large and thriving Dominican population. But after a brief stay in the Big Apple, they decided to move to Independence, a small Missouri town that sits on the south bank of the Missouri River. Located a few miles east of Kansas City, Independence is best known as the childhood hometown of Harry S. Truman, the thirty-third President of the United States.

TWO

The Crack of Thunder

Soon after arriving in Independence, Albert began attending Fort Osage High School. Although he would have been entering his junior year had he remained in the DR, Albert was registered as a sophomore, because he spoke very little English. So, in addition to having to adjust to a big move and a different culture, Albert also had to learn how to read and speak an entirely new language.

Albert worked very hard at increasing his vocabulary and mastering the use of English, which is a difficult language to learn. But he stepped up to the challenge in the same energetic way that he swings at a 95-miles-per-hour fastball.

"He was a very willing student," said Portia Stanke, who was Albert's language tutor during the two-and-a-half years that he spent at Fort Osage High School. "He was dedicated about learning the language, and always very well prepared."

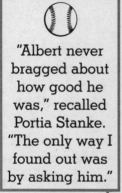

"Albert never bragged about how good he was," recalled Portia Stanke. "The only way I found out was by asking him."

Although he did very well in the classroom, by the time the calendar turned to February, Albert was chafing at the bit for the chance to try out for the school's baseball team. And from Albert's first few swings, Dave Fry, who was the baseball coach at the time, knew that he might have someone special in his lineup for the 1997 season.

"I wasn't even watching him hit at first," recalled Fry. "But the sound of the bat on the ball certainly caught my attention, and made me turn around very quickly. The sound was explosive, like the crack of thunder, and it was just as startling. I just looked at him and thought, 'He looks like a man playing against boys.'"

Albert had no trouble making the starting lineup as the team's shortstop, and even though he hadn't yet mastered English, Coach Fry never had any problem communicating with his star pupil.

"Even though I didn't speak Spanish and Albert hadn't, as yet, become fluent in English, I was always able to communicate exactly what I wanted him to do," said Coach Fry. "Whether it was how I wanted him to position himself in the field, or how to move his hands when he was at-bat, there was never a problem. He held the bat a bit higher than I thought was optimum, and I suggested that he lower his hands a little. That was about as far as it went. He had such a deep under-

> "I heard a sound that sounded like, 'whack, whack, whack,'" said coach Dave Fry. "I had never heard anything like it."

standing of the game that I didn't have to do a great deal of instructing. He was just a natural-born baseball player."

Albert also had such a great passion for playing baseball that it almost seemed as if the game provided him with the very fuel of life. That desire, coupled with superior talent, allowed Albert to hit for a .471 average, drill 11 dingers, rack up 32 RBI, and lead the Indians to the 1997 Missouri Class 4A championship.

"I want to be a consistent and complete player. I don't want people saying, 'He's a great hitter, but he can't play in the field.'"

"That was an amazing feeling," recalled Albert. "To come to America and help my team win a championship that first year. It doesn't get much better than that."

The following year, opposing pitchers showed that they didn't want any part of Albert by walking him a staggering 55 times in his 88 at-bats. Albert was thoroughly frustrated at having the bat taken out of his hands so frequently, but he refused to swing at wayward pitches. His willingness to be disciplined and not swing at pitches out of the strike zone was remarkable for such a young hitter. It's a trait that he has carried into his major league career, and that has helped him to become one of those rare players who not only hit for power, but for a high batting average, as well.

"He's such a complete player," said Cardinals manager Tony La Russa. "I've often told him, 'I'd like to meet the person who taught you how to play.'"

When pitchers did challenge Albert, he made them pay for their bravery by hammering eight homers, averaging nearly one big fly for every four at-bats. Albert showed that he had prime-time power by not merely hitting home runs, but by hitting balls so far that they seemed to defy gravity, including one that Coach Fry recalled as if it had happened yesterday.

"He hit the ball so hard, so high that it cleared the left field fence and landed on top of an air conditioning unit that was on the roof of a building," recalled Fry. "That ball had to travel 450 feet, but while it was in the air, I didn't think it was ever going to come down."

Despite Albert's prowess at the plate, major league scouts didn't rate him very highly, because he made a bunch of errors at shortstop and was slow getting down the line to first base.

"He would keep me hitting ground balls to him until my shoulders were too sore to swing the bat," said Dave Fry.

"He certainly had the size and strength," noted Mike Roberts, a scout for the St. Louis Cardinals. "But he was by no means the type of player that had a 'can't-miss' tag on him."

To improve his chances of being drafted by a major league team, some scouts advised Albert to graduate high school early, so that he could play for a junior college team, where he would have more of an opportunity to impress scouts by facing hurlers who wouldn't be afraid of pitching to him.

THREE

The Sound of Cannons

Albert took the advice and, in January of 1999, he enrolled at Maple Woods Community College, a few miles away from home in Kansas City. Once again, it took only a single batting practice session to convince people that Albert was not an ordinary hitter.

"I was feeling pretty good about my session," said Landon Brandes, who was a year ahead of Albert and the team's top hitter. "I put more than a few balls over the fence but, like everyone else, I was using an aluminum bat. Then Albert steps in, using a wooden bat, and proceeds to hit balls that made my blasts look skimpy. It was a humbling moment."

Albert continued to shine when the real games started, as he stoked a grand slam and turned an unassisted triple play in the first game of the Centaurs' season. Then, he went and showed that that per-formance wasn't just begin-ner's luck by slugging 22 homers and knocking in 76 runs in 56 games, while post-ing a .466 batting average and a .953 slugging percent-age, all of which set single-season school records.

"I've never met anybody else who had so much talent, drive, and determination to get better," said Marty Kilgore.

"He obviously had tre-mendous power and a great eye, but it wasn't just his hitting that impressed me," said Marty Kilgore, who was Albert's coach at Maple Woods. "He was an excel-lent and aggressive base-runner, who knew how and when to take an extra base. He did all the little things that are telltale signs of exceptional baseball intelligence. He was, without a doubt, the finest athlete I've ever seen or coached."

With Albert's king-sized help, the Centaurs captured the 1999 National Junior College Athletic Association regional championship, and fell only one game short of making it to the Junior College World Series.

Despite Albert's accomplishments and Coach Kilgore's appraisal, most major league scouts remained unimpressed with Albert's potential to play in the big leagues. Some of the scouts questioned the accuracy of his arm, while others were concerned that he hadn't spent enough time developing his upper-body strength. One exception to the prevailing opinion was that of Fernando Arango, who was a scout for the Tampa Bay Devil Rays.

"What I saw in him was tremendous athletic ability," said Arango. "He just hit the ball with an impact that you don't see every day. I went to a game at Maple Woods when he cracked two home runs, and the sound of the bat on the balls sounded like cannon shots."

Arango's reports created enough enthusiasm for the Devil Rays front office to fly Albert to Tampa Bay's Tropicana Field for a tryout shortly before the 1999 amateur draft. But Albert didn't do anything to impress Dan Jennings who, at the time, was the D-Rays director of scouting.

"He didn't put a single ball into the stands, and only one even reached the warning track," recalled Jennings. "He didn't do anything to indicate that he could even make the majors, let alone become a great player."

When the draft took place that June, Albert was ignored by every team, round after round, until the Cardinals picked him in the 13th round, after 401 other players—most of whom would wind up having to pay their way into a major league stadium—had been selected. Right after the draft, Arango was so angered that the D-Rays didn't draft Albert that he quit his job.

"I was so frustrated," recalled Arango, who went on to become the coordinator of Latin American Scouting for the Milwaukee Brewers. "To me it was very simple: If I can't get a guy like that, even in the 10th round, maybe I need to be somewhere where my recommendations are more respected."

With the benefit of hindsight, Jennings, at least, has learned from his mistake, and now puts more weight on the advice of scouts when they are passionate about prospects.

"That was my guy," said Ernie Jacobs, a Boston scout, who couldn't convince the Red Sox to draft Albert. "I lost my Hall of Famer."

"That was absolutely the biggest mistake we made when I was in Tampa Bay," said Jennings, who went on to become the

Player Personnel Director of the Florida Marlins. "For a while, I just thought I was hexed. Every time I'd turn on a TV when he came up with the Cardinals he would be hitting a home run or driving in the winning run. I'd look up and say, 'I get the message.' You can make one bad decision and it can bite you forever. If we had picked him even as low as the ninth round, we'd look like geniuses."

Albert was already annoyed at being drafted with such a low pick, and the Cardinals didn't do anything to make him feel any better when Dave Karaff, the scout who went to sign him, offered only $10,000 as a signing bonus.

"It did bother me," recalled Albert. "I was terribly disappointed and even thought that maybe I should quit baseball."

Instead of quitting, however, Albert went to play in the Jayhawk League, a summer league for college-aged players, and he did so well that by the end of the 1999 season the Cardinals decided to up their offer to $65,000, which included salary for the 2000 season, a signing bonus, and money set aside for Albert to attend college. It would turn out to be the best deal that the team ever made, but the events surrounding the episode have continued to spur Albert on to greatness.

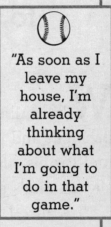

"As soon as I leave my house, I'm already thinking about what I'm going to do in that game."

"All that stays with him, absolutely," noted Scott Mihlfeld, a friend and trainer who works with Albert in the off-season. "Albert is a hard-headed guy. He does not forget. He doesn't hold grudges, but there is no question that being drafted low and having the Cardinals come in with a low-ball offer motivates him every day."

FOUR

On a Fast Track
to the Big Time

While Albert has used his experience with the draft and the Cards' initial low-ball offer as fuel for his success, he quickly resolved not to allow other's people opinions to lay him low.

"I realized that it didn't really matter how I was rated at the time," said Albert, who just wanted to start making his way up through the Cardinals' system. "I knew if I was good enough, I would make it to the big leagues in three or four years."

Albert's road to St. Louis started in the fall of 1999, in Jupiter, Florida, where the Cardinals field a team in the Instructional League. Once again, Albert made an amazing first impression, this time on Cardinals' executive and former big league first baseman, Mike Jorgensen, who watched the young slugger slash a line drive well beyond the left field wall and crash the wall with two other drives. After a few more days of watching Albert tattoo the outfield fences, he wondered why the Cards' scouts hadn't rated him more highly.

"I know that some of them had doubts about his speed and physique, but it didn't take a telescope to see that his bat speed was exceptional," recalled Jorgensen. "Everyone missed the boat on Albert, and we were just lucky to have anchored him in the 13th round. In fact, we would have been lucky and looked a whole lot smarter if we had

"His super-strong hands and extraordinary eye-hand coordination are the secrets to his success," noted Tom Lawless.

picked Prince Albert in the first round."

After a successful mini-season in the Instructional League, where Albert started to learn how to play third base, he went home for the winter. Albert spent those few months working out and earning money at a temporary job, and he also took a huge step in his young life when he married his girlfriend of the past year, Deidre, on New Year's Day of 2000, and adopted her infant daughter, Isabella, who had been born with Down Syndrome.

Although people many years older than Albert, who was 19 at the time, would have run the other way when they found out that a woman had a child with such a severe illness, Albert had the wisdom and maturity to look beyond the disease and see the person.

"Once he figured it out—and he figured it real fast—there wasn't any doubt that he would hit in the big leagues," said Lawless.

"I never really gave it a thought," said Albert, who has gone on to have two other children with his wife. "I loved Deidre and I loved Isabella. It was as simple as that."

When it was time for Albert to report for spring training, he was assigned to Peoria (Illinois), the Cardinals' low-level Class-A team in the Midwest League. It didn't take long for Albert to make the adjustment to playing against other professionals or to catch the eye of his manager, Tom Lawless, a former big league infielder.

"He needed to work on his defense, which he did with great diligence," said Lawless. "But it was clear from the get-go that he was a superior hitter. For one thing, he had great mechanics, and he also seemed mature beyond his years. Most power hitters try to pull everything, no matter where the pitch is thrown. But whenever Albert got a pitch from the middle of the plate on out, he would go with the pitch and hit the ball to right or right center.

"After the other teams figured out what he was about, they had their pitchers try to get him out by jamming him with inside pitches. That was effective for a short time, but we taught him how to generate more bat speed through the strike zone, and in no time, he was turning on those inside pitches and racking up extra-base hits to left and left center. At that point, it must have been pretty discouraging to be standing on the mound when Albert stepped into the batter's box."

Despite his rapid adjustment to professional pitching, Albert wasn't satisfied, and when Mitchell Page, who was the Cardinals' league hitting instructor, showed up in Peoria, Albert was the first one to seek him out.

"He wasn't happy hitting just because he was hitting over .300, so I gave him all the extra work he wanted," said Page, smiling at the memory. "But he was already an A+ student, and I really didn't have too much more knowledge of the art of hitting than he already had."

Albert wound up playing in 109 games for the Chiefs, and posted a .324 average, hammered 17 homers and racked up 84 RBI in 89 games, while striking out only 37 times in 395 at-bats. But it wasn't just his hitting that caught the eye of his coaches and teammates.

Albert was chosen as the Midwest League's All-Star third baseman, and was named the league's MVP, despite missing the last month of the season.

"Everyone who saw Albert play knew that he was a special talent," said Albert's Peoria teammate, Ben Johnson, a fourth round pick who was soon traded to the San Diego Padres, and will play for the New York Mets in 2007. "He was a great third baseman—the best in the league we played in, *by far.* A lot of people don't know how good an athlete Albert is. He can play basketball, too. He can do anything, really. More importantly, he was a wonderful teammate."

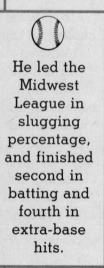

He led the Midwest League in slugging percentage, and finished second in batting and fourth in extra-base hits.

Albert's stellar play earned him an August promotion to Potomac, which was the Cardinals' higher-level Class-A team in the Carolina League. Albert played in 21 games for the Cannons, who are based in Virginia, and hit for a .284 average.

"He hit the ball harder and more often than anyone I had ever seen," said former Cannons' teammate Bo Hart. "Even when he made an out, it was simply because he had happened to hit a line drive right at a fielder, not because the pitcher had overpowered him."

When an opening developed on the

Cardinals' Triple-A team in Memphis (Tennessee), the Redbirds' manager asked the organization to send him the young phenom he had heard so much about.

"They were a little reluctant at first," recalled Gaylen Pitts, who was the Redbirds' manager at the time. "But we were about to start the Pacific Coast League (PCL) playoffs, and we had room for a right-handed hitter."

It was decided that Albert would be given a few days to try to adapt to pitchers who were only one rung below the big league level. If he was successful, he would be put on the Redbirds' postseason roster; if he wasn't, he'd sit on the sidelines until play began in the Arizona Fall League. Just to complicate matters for Albert, he was asked to play left field, a position he'd never played before, after he'd spent the entire season at the hot corner.

Albert not only passed his tryout test,

but went on to post a .302 average during the postseason and .367, with a pair of homers and five RBI, in the seven-game PCL playoffs. Albert, in fact, put a dramatic exclamation mark on the playoff series when he hit the game-winning, 13th-inning home run that delivered the PCL championship to the Redbirds. The series-clinching big fly also clinched the series MVP award for Albert.

Albert, actually, won a host of postseason awards, including three from Baseball America, which named him the Midwest League's best batting prospect, top defensive third baseman, and the owner of the best arm among the league's infielders.

Then, Albert topped off his amazing ride through the Cardinals' farm system by hitting .323 and rapping 21 RBI in just 27 games in the Arizona Fall League, and was voted the third-best prospect in that league by the circuit's coaches and managers.

"He was a kind of one-man wrecking crew," noted Mike Jorgensen. "At that point, it was obvious to me that he was going to be a special kind of player, and not just a top-notch hitter."

After watching Albert climb the rungs of their minor league ladder, the Cardinals told him that they were going to invite him to spring training in 2001, which is something that big league teams sometimes do to give their hot prospects a small, if usually temporary, taste of life on a big league level. When Albert shared that news with Marty Kilgore, his

> "Playing in the minors was a lot of fun, even the 10-hour bus rides, but after a taste of the majors, I didn't want to go back there."

former coach kidded him about how neat it would be to be throwing balls to Mark McGwire, who had hit 70 home runs in 1998, during infield drills.

"I mean, no one expected Albert to

make the jump to the Cardinals after only one season in the minors, it just doesn't happen that way," explained Kilgore. "But Albert just looked at me with a very determined stare and said, 'I am not going there to throw to Mark McGwire. I'm going there to make the team.'"

FIVE

Rookie of the Year

Because money was tight, Albert spent the winter working in the catering department of a local country club, and he, Deidre, and Isabella moved in with his in-laws, so that the couple could save money on rent. The extra money became even more necessary in January, when Deidre gave birth to a son, Alberto, Junior, who was quickly nicknamed A.J.

Between his job and the responsibilities of family life, Albert still managed to carve out a significant amount of time to work out and to hone his baseball skills. He knew that if he was going to have any chance to go north with the Cardinals, he would have to come to spring training in prime-time shape and get off to a quick start. He knew that the organization wasn't going to invest too many at-bats in a player with only one year of professional ball under his belt—unless that player did things that forced them to pay attention to him.

"He's focused in everything he does, from hitting to running down the line," said Hall of Famer Red Schoendienst. "He doesn't just go through the motions."

When Albert arrived at the Cardinals' spring training site in Jupiter, Florida, he was given No. 68, a sure sign that the Cardinals didn't expect him to be around very long. But Albert started changing the basis of that assumption from the very first swings he took in the batting cage.

"He was taking really professional at-bats," said Cards' pitching coach Dave Duncan. "You could tell that he was determined to compete from the moment he took his first practice swings. Even though it was only batting practice in February, he treated every at-bat as though it was a game-winning situation in the regular season. He didn't waste any swings, or chase after bad pitches. He had a very disciplined and mature approach to hitting, which really caught my eye."

At that point, however, it seemed as though there wasn't anything that Albert could do to crack the Cards' veteran lineup. He was so far out of their plans, in fact, that Cards' manager Tony La Russa didn't even assign Albert a permanent position and, instead, kept moving him around the diamond, playing him not only at third base, but also at first, shortstop, and in the outfield, as well.

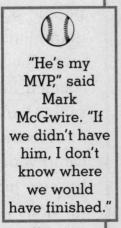

"He's my MVP," said Mark McGwire. "If we didn't have him, I don't know where we would have finished."

"It was obvious that he had a lot of talent, and I thought that he had a chance to make it to the bigs," said La Russa. "But I didn't think there was any way that he was going to do it without a full year in Triple-A, so I just used him to fill in wherever I needed him."

Albert, however, had other plans, and his hitting and play on the field started to make La Russa have second thoughts about sending him back to Memphis. Albert had also caught the attention of people outside the organization, like veteran manager Felipe Alou.

"I saw a lot of Albert that spring, and it seemed like everything he hit was *hard*," said Alou, whose team at the time, the Montreal Expos, shared the Jupiter training camp with St. Louis. "It really surprised me to see a hitter who had been at Class-A the previous year develop so quickly."

Albert made the decision to send him back to Triple-A a hard one, by leading the club in total bases, and posting a .349 average, with only eight strikeouts in 62 at-bats. Those numbers and his hard work prolonged Albert's stay with the Cards, but he was still ticketed for a return ride to Memphis until Bobby Bonilla, a Cards' outfielder, suffered an injury toward the end of spring training. And even when La Russa told Albert that he would be starting the season with St. Louis, he tempered the good news by telling him that he would probably be sent down after the team's opening series in Colorado.

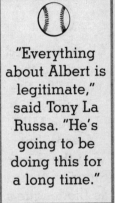

"Everything about Albert is legitimate," said Tony La Russa. "He's going to be doing this for a long time."

"I was fortunate enough to get a chance to make the team," said Albert, who was assigned No. 5. "But that wouldn't have mattered if I didn't believe that I *could* make the team."

Cards' general manager Walt Jocketty decided that Albert was not only up for good, but that he had such vast potential that he should be given a "significant" number, which to Jocketty meant a single digit number.

Albert finished fourth in the voting for the National League MVP Award, but won the Silver Slugger Award as the league's best-hitting third baseman.

"You look at the ones we've retired—Stan Musial, Red Schoendienst, Ozzie Smith—they're single digits," noted Jocketty, speaking of three of the team's Hall of Famers. "It's hard to explain, but I think they look better."

Albert, playing left field and batting sixth, singled on Opening Day against the Rockies, and even though that was the only hit he recorded in the three-game series, he wasn't at all discouraged or intimidated by big league pitching.

"I hit the ball hard, so I didn't get frustrated," explained Albert. "I knew what I could do."

Albert showed just what he could do in

the team's next series, when he scorched Arizona Diamondback pitchers for seven hits in 14 at-bats, and racked up a pair of homers and eight RBI. One of Albert's hits was a two-strike, two-run double against Arizona ace, Randy Johnson, who would go on to win the 2001 National League (NL) Cy Young Award, the third in his string of four straight Cy Young Awards.

"When he rocked that double off of Randy Johnson, everyone in the dugout opened their eyes wide," said former teammate, Mark McGwire. "Right there, we knew we had a hitter."

Due to injuries to McGwire and others, La Russa was forced to move Albert up two spaces in the batting order, which put him in the clean-up position. Managers don't like to put a young player in the position of being

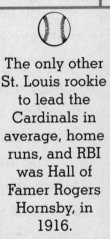

The only other St. Louis rookie to lead the Cardinals in average, home runs, and RBI was Hall of Famer Rogers Hornsby, in 1916.

expected to be a team's No. 1 run produc-
er. They also don't like to distract players,
especially young ones, by moving them
around on the field, but La Russa moved
Albert all over the diamond, depending
upon who else was available to play. But
neither the batting order change, nor the
constant change in positions affected
Albert, who acted as if he didn't have a
nerve in his body.

"You see a lot of rookies who look over-
matched at this level," said Bob Brenly,
who was the Diamondbacks' manager.
"Other rookies have a look in their eyes
that lets you know they think that they
belong. Albert certainly has that look."

During his first month in the majors,
Albert ripped National League pitchers for
a .370 average, racked up 27 RBI in 24
games, and hit eight homers, which tied
the major-league record for homers by a
rookie in April.

Albert continued on his torrid pace through the first three months of the 2001 season, before he suffered through a 2-for-33 slump in early July. But he came into the mid-point of the season among the league leaders in most every hitting category, and was selected to play in the All-Star Game, a rare honor for a first-year player.

Albert became just the fourth rookie in major league history to hit at least .300, score 100 runs, rap 30 homers, and knock in 100 runs.

As the season turned to the dog days of August, Albert heated up, as he went on a 17-game hitting streak, and helped lead the Cards to within six games of the Central Division lead.

Albert was already a lock for the NL Rookie of the Year award, but a number of people started touting him as an MVP contender, including Mark McGwire.

"There's no doubt in my mind that if we make the playoffs, Albert should be an MVP candidate," said Big Mac. "He respects everyone and everything about the game, but this kid isn't in awe of anything or anyone."

The Cards closed with a rush in September, and finished in a tie with the Houston Astros for the division title with a 93–69 record. The Cards, however, came up a game short in the opening round of the playoffs, losing 3-games-to-2 to the Diamondbacks, who went on to win a classic World Series against the New York Yankees. Albert, who collected only two hits in 18 at-bats, didn't do much to help the Cardinals' cause, but nothing that happened in the postseason could diminish his astonishing record-setting accomplishments during the regular season.

In his first season in the big leagues, Albert set National League rookie marks for RBI (130), extra-base hits (88) and total bases (360), and became only the second

Cardinal rookie to lead the team in RBI, home runs (37), and average (.329).

"For Albert to do what he did for six months is just phenomenal," said La Russa. "If he had been a 10-year veteran, it still would have been exceptional, but to have done it in his rookie season is just unheard of."

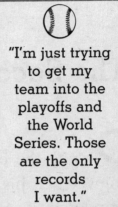

"I'm just trying to get my team into the playoffs and the World Series. Those are the only records I want."

The Baseball Writers of America agreed, and selected Albert as the winner of the National League Rookie of the Year Award by a unanimous vote.

"It's nice to be recognized," said Albert. "But I don't think about awards and records. I just want to help my team win, and we came up a little bit short this year."

SIX

The Second Time Around

Despite the enormous success that he had enjoyed in his rookie season, people still wondered if Albert would succumb to the dreaded 'sophomore slump', a second-year fall-off in production that had snared so many other players before him.

Albert, however, took steps to avoid that fate by diligently working out through the off-season, and by watching countless hours of videotape of opposing pitchers, as he prepared himself for the 2002 season. Albert's mindset was also important, as he refused to bask in his past accomplishments. If he turned out to be another flash-in-the-pan, it wouldn't be because of any complacency on his part.

"It's not what you did last year that counts," declared Albert, at the start of spring training. "It's what you're going to do this year. That's more important.

"I don't want to throw this opportunity away," he added. "I don't want to be lazy or take things for granted. I don't want to be cocky and think I'm the best. I want to stay humble and keep working as hard as I can, so I can get as good as I can."

"I don't believe in jinxes. I believe in hard work and preparing myself to play the best that I can, so that I can help my team win."

Albert's approach and work habits were noted by his teammates and the coaching staff, who appreciated his dedication and determination to succeed at a very high level.

"He works harder now than he did as a rookie," noted Tony La Russa. "And it was his work ethic, more than his talent, which won him the respect of the veterans on this club when he first came to spring training last year."

In addition to studying opposing pitchers, Albert also took every opportunity to study the other top hitters in the game, seeing if there was anything that he could learn from them and adapt for his own use.

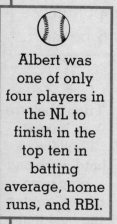

Albert was one of only four players in the NL to finish in the top ten in batting average, home runs, and RBI.

"I learn so much by watching great hitters, such as Todd Helton and Alex Rodriguez," explained Albert. "They've been successful for a lot longer than I have, so I'd have to be pretty stupid or arrogant to think that I couldn't benefit from watching the way they approach different pitchers and situations.

"I'm a really smart player," continued Albert. "If you tell me something, I get it quickly. If there is something wrong with my hitting, tell me what's wrong and I'll pick it up right away. That's the best thing I have going for me, my ability to listen to a coach and fix what I'm doing wrong."

Albert's willingness to learn from more veteran players and his coaches set him apart from some other players, especially young players, who felt that they already knew everything there was to know.

"He has the best work habits I've ever seen in a young kid," said Mitchell Page, the Cardinals' former hitting coach. "He takes nothing for granted.

"Left-hander, right-hander, soft tosser, power pitcher, fast balls away, fast balls in—he doesn't have any holes," said former teammate Tino Martinez.

But his work doesn't stop when he puts the bat down. He's constantly trying to improve as a fielder, and he's always asking questions, always trying to take it to the next level."

Unlike the previous year, Albert didn't

jump out to a fast start, because opposing scouts and pitchers found holes in his swing and worked on those weaknesses. But Albert countered their moves by making his own adjustments through watching himself on videotape in the clubhouse after every at-bat.

"That's how you become a good hitter," explained Albert, who also worked tirelessly in the batting cage. "You don't want to have three bad at-bats and then try to figure it out. You want to make adjustments after your first at-bat."

Any thought that Albert might be swallowed by a sophomore slump were put to rest by a second-half surge, starting in August, when he drove in 32 runs and hit for a .368 average.

"I wasn't concerned that it took awhile to get my average up above .300," said Albert. "I was driving in runs and helping my team win, and that's always the bottom line for me. I worked hard and, like I've always known, if I work hard, good things are going to happen."

Albert's calm reaction to relative adversity is one of the backbones of his personality, a quality that allows him to face up to a challenge, instead of allowing it to overwhelm him.

"I don't put pressure on myself," said Albert. "I just concentrate on what I need to do, and do it the best I can. I make it a habit to do my best every day, and help my team to win any way I can."

For the second year in a row, Albert completed the team Triple Crown by leading the Cardinals in average, RBI, and home runs.

Albert's ability to block out pressure in a sport where pitchers are throwing the ball 95-mph and 40,000 people are clamoring for or against him, depending upon whether he's playing at home or away, has gained him many fans within the game.

"He stands like a man," said former San Francisco Giants' manager, Felipe Alou. "They didn't teach him fear where he grew up. It's not part of his bag."

It certainly didn't hurt Albert's ability to pile up hits when the Cardinals made a blockbuster trade with the Philadelphia Phillies on July 29 that brought Scott Rolen to the team. With Rolen's big bat hitting behind him, pitchers became less likely to pitch around Albert, and more likely to put pitches in the strike zone. The addition of Rolen, a perennial Gold Glove third baseman, also meant that Albert had one less fielder's mitt to keep in his locker.

"He has a knack for controlling the at-bat," said Jim Edmonds, "rather than allowing the pitcher to take control of it."

While Rolen certainly strengthened the Cardinals' offense and provided protection behind Albert in the lineup, the Cards' new third baseman also got to appreciate just how talented his new teammate was.

"You see him twice a year and you fig-ure you're catching him when he's hot," said Rolen. "When you're on the same team, you realize he's like that every day. You think he has to cool off sometimes, but he doesn't. He's that good."

With Albert, Rolen, and cen-ter fielder Jim Edmonds, a left-handed hitter, supplying the muscle, and closer Jason Isring-hausen anchoring the bullpen, the Cards ran away from their divisional rivals and copped the Central Division crown with a 97–65 record.

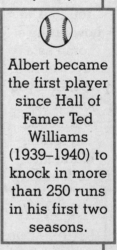

Albert became the first player since Hall of Famer Ted Williams (1939–1940) to knock in more than 250 runs in his first two seasons.

Their opening round playoff opponent was, once again, the Arizona Diamond-backs, but this time the Cards shuffled the deck and swept the series, 3–0. Their next opponent was the San Francisco Giants, and the series was billed as a battle of the superstars, with Albert sharing the stage with Barry Bonds, who had led the majors with a .370 batting average. Neither player produced the fireworks that were anticipated, but the Giants took the NL pennant, 3-games-to-2, denying Albert and his teammates a chance to play in the 2002 World Series.

Albert, who finished the season with a .314 average (a career *low*), 34 homers, 127 RBI, and 118 runs scored, also came in second behind Bonds in voting for the NL MVP Award. But neither the loss in the postseason, nor the one in the voting could dim the luster from his regular season performance, as Albert continued to build on his spectacular rookie year by becoming the first player in big league history to hit at least .300

> "You look at how far he's come as a player in two years, and you just shake your head," said former teammate Mike Matheny.

with 30 homers, 100 RBI, and 100 runs scored in each of his first two seasons.

"He is the whole package," declared Tony La Russa. "There's going to be a time when we all look back and say, 'Wow, we got to see that man play early in his career, before he became a legend.'"

SEVEN

Hitting New Heights

In each of his first two seasons in the big leagues, Albert had already put up numbers that most players can only dream about. But for Albert, they were just an appetizer for what he was about to accomplish in the 2003 season.

As he had in his rookie season, Albert got off to a quick start when he hit for a .385 average in April, and then turned May into a merry month, indeed, by clubbing 10 round-trippers, and racking up 26 RBI.

"I've managed my share of outstanding players, from Ricky Henderson to Mark McGwire, but Albert is the best of all," said Tony La Russa.

"I know that it's only the start of his third season, but I've already seen enough."

Albert continued to rock the ball throughout the spring and early summer, as he posted a .429 average with 29 RBI in June, and headed to the halfway point of the season as the hottest hitter in baseball. In a season of memorable at-bats, some people point to a July 4th match-up against the Chicago Cubs' flame-thrower, Kerry Wood, whose heater tops out in the 100-mph range, as one of Albert's signature moments.

As the hot summer sun poured down on Wrigley Field, Wood put Albert on his backside with a 98-mph two-seam fastball that all but shaved some of the hair off Albert's chin.

In an age when too many players are too quick to charge the mound or scream

"I've played with great players, guys who put up some good numbers," said Tino Martinez. "But I've never seen a guy as focused as he is. He's just amazing."

curses at pitchers who pitch tight, Albert just stood up and stepped back into the batter's box. Then he crushed Wood's next pitch over the ivy-covered wall, a blast that helped the Cards topple the Cubs.

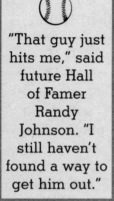

"That guy just hits me," said future Hall of Famer Randy Johnson. "I still haven't found a way to get him out."

"You don't rattle him," said Jim Edmonds afterwards. "He rattles you."

Albert's first-half exploits caused the fans around the country to mark their ballot boxes for him, making him the top vote-getter in the National League All-Star Game. And while Albert was having a blast visiting with the other major league stars, and coming in second in the Home Run Derby behind Garret Anderson of the California Angels, Tony La Russa was having his moments of satisfaction, too.

"I had a couple of guys from the American League who had challenged my statement that Albert was the best player I had ever managed," said La Russa. "But after the All-Star Game they told me, 'We thought when you said that you were just exaggerating to make a point. But now we understand what you were talking about. He's an *awesome* talent.'"

> "I want to be in the lineup every day. Playing somewhere is better than sitting on the bench."

The people who were around Albert the most knew that his high level of talent was only half the story in his rapid rise to superstar status. Although Albert is blessed with a great deal of natural talent, so are many people who don't make it past their local street corners; people who don't have the discipline to develop their talent or the good sense to not get involved with drugs and other criminal activity. Deion Sanders, the former NFL All-Pro cornerback invented a special name for people like them.

"Let me tell you something," said Sanders, who grew up in a crime- and drug-infested neighborhood, but was strong enough and smart enough to avoid the abyss, and had the dedication to show up at practice every day. *"The best athletes in the world end up on the corner.* Oh, you bet they do. I call them *Idas.* 'If *I'da* done this, *I'da* been here today, just like you, Deion. If *I'da* done that, I'd be making three million dollars a year. If *I'da* practiced a little bit harder, I'd be a superstar, too.'"

But as Deion knew, those people never do practice harder or make the big money, and the only place they ever get to be a superstar is in their own wasted minds.

"I see them all the time; guys who were as fast as I was when we were kids," added Deion, who was the fastest player in the NFL. "They'll be standing on that corner until the day they die, telling you the things they *could* have done."

Unlike the *Idas*, no one has ever had to tell Albert to practice more or stay away from drugs. From high school to the big leagues, Albert has worn out coaches and batting practice pitchers, doing everything he can to take his talent to the limit.

"I've never seen a young player as disciplined as he is," said Mitchell Page, who was the Cardinals' hitting instructor at the time. "He constantly watches video, and everything he does has a purpose, there's no downtime with Albert. You watch him, even in the pre-game drills, and you see how determined he is. He learned a hitting drill from A-Rod, where he hits off a tee, just to make sure that he keeps his stroke level and doesn't develop any bad habits.

"And the reality of it is, his swing is a

"He's one of those rare guys who hits for power and average and doesn't strike out much," said veteran hurler Tom Glavine.

thing of beauty," continued Page, who went on to compare Albert's stroke to those of a trio of Hall of Famers. "I look at his swing and I think of names like Ted Williams, Rod Carew, and George Brett, guys who had beautiful swings. It's a gift, and that type of gift doesn't come around very often."

"He's the entire package," said Tony La Russa. "He commits to defense just like he does to offense."

Although the Cardinals faded from the playoff race in September, when their fragile pitching staff broke down, Albert continued to manhandle opposing pitchers through the end of the season, and continued to establish himself as one of the most dominant hitters in the game. Albert, in fact, led all major leaguers in six offensive categories, including batting average (.359); runs scored (137); doubles (51); extra-base hits (95); and total bases (394). His phenomenal performance, which also included 43 homers, 124 RBI, 212 hits, and only 65 strikeouts, was one of the finest ever compiled by any player in the long and storied history of the St. Louis Cardinals. In fact, only one other Cardinal, Rogers Hornsby, ever hit 40 or more homers and collected at least 200 hits in the same season.

At 23, Albert had become the youngest player to win a batting title since 1962, when Los Angeles Dodgers' outfielder Tommy Davis accomplished the same feat when he, too, was 23 years old.

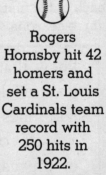

Rogers Hornsby hit 42 homers and set a St. Louis Cardinals team record with 250 hits in 1922.

Although Albert finished second behind Barry Bonds in the voting for the MVP Award, the players in the game disagreed with the Baseball Writer's Association of America (BBWAA) and selected him as the winner of the Players' Choice Major League Player of the Year Award, and also chose him as the National League's Outstanding Player.

During his first three years in the majors, Albert had put up numbers which favorably compared with the best career starts of all-time, and his 114 home runs tied Hall of Famer Ralph Kiner's major league record for the most homers hit in a player's first trio of seasons. Albert knew that he had already accomplished a great deal, but he also realized that he still had miles to go.

Albert is one of only three players to hit 30 or more home runs in each of his first three seasons.

"Of course I want to be considered one of the game's best players when I retire from baseball," said Albert, who made only three errors during the 2003 season, while playing 113 games in left field and 36 at first base. "I want to play well enough to make it to the Hall of Fame. But we're a long way from there, and I still have a lot more to accomplish."

EIGHT

A Step Away

The Cardinals organization thought so highly of Albert's potential that, in February of 2004, they signed him to a franchise-record, seven-year, $100 million contract, the highest amount ever paid to any third-year player. Although some people wondered if such an enormous guaranteed contract might make him complacent, Albert assured everyone that the money wasn't going to change his approach or attitude.

"I will keep working hard, both mentally and physically, because I know if you feel too comfortable, that's when someone comes from the minor leagues and takes your spot," said Albert.

"I came out of nowhere and took some-one's job, and someone else can come along and do the same to me, if I slack off."

Albert had taken an amazing journey, from a childhood fraught with poverty and uncertainty in the Dominican Republic, to a life that was filled with astonishing amounts of money and the security of a loving family. In achieving the heights that he had, Albert had also accepted and embraced his responsibility to act as a positive model for all the fans that followed his career.

"I want to make sure that I'm a role model not just for the Latin people, but for the American people, too."

"I hope I'm a role model for the millions of people who come to this country with the same dreams that my family had," said Albert. "But I also want to be a role model for everyone, no matter where they were born, or what the color of their skin is. When I walk out of the game, I want to be remembered as one of the best players, but I also want people to remember me as one of the best people; as someone who respected my fans and gave something back to them."

Although Albert would certainly have liked to begin the 2004 season with a bang after signing that big-bucks contract, he got off to a slow start due, at least in part, to a strained hamstring muscle. But by the middle of May, as the weather turned warm and the hamstring healed, Albert started to heat up, and as the calendar turned to July, he went on a sizzling three-month season-ending tear, during which he hit .359.

As a team, the Cardinals also got off to a sluggish start, but then, almost in lockstep with Albert's up-tick, they started to surge, and finished the season as the Central Division champions.

Although Albert, who played his first

full season at first base, was the center-
piece of the team, Cardinals' general manager Walt Jocketty had assembled an
offensive juggernaut that led the league in
batting average; runs scored; RBI; and slugging percentage, and finished third in home runs, with 214.

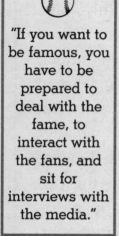

"If you want to be famous, you have to be prepared to deal with the fame, to interact with the fans, and sit for interviews with the media."

Jim Edmonds—who matched his career high with 42 home runs, and posted a career-best 111 RBI—and Scott Rolen—who set career highs with 34 big flies and 124 RBI—were the other big run-producers.

Left fielder Reggie Sanders also supplied a
potent bat, while second baseman Tony
Womack and shortstop Edgar Renteria
were at the top of Tony La Russa's batting
order, where they set the table for the big
boppers who followed. Jocketty completed this star-studded cast via an August

trade with the Colorado Rockies that landed right fielder Larry Walker, a former
league MVP and batting title-winner.

The Cardinals also had a better-than-
average pitching staff, which
was led by starters Chris Carpenter, Jeff Suppan, and Jason
Marquis, and closer Jason
Isringhausen, who tied for the
league lead with 47 saves.

Albert had what was com-
ing to be thought of as his
usual season of brilliance, as

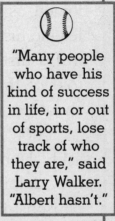

"Many people
who have his
kind of success
in life, in or out
of sports, lose
track of who
they are," said
Larry Walker.
"Albert hasn't."

he finished among the league leaders in
every major offensive category, and led
the majors in runs, total bases, and extra-
base hits.

"He's unbelievable," said Scott Rolen.
"He's on it 162 games a year. I've never
seen anyone else like him. I'm lucky if I'm
on it for 100 games...or for that matter, 62
games."

Albert also continued to generate career stats that placed him alongside the all-time greats of the game, such as Hall of Famers Joe DiMaggio and Ted Williams, whom he joined as the only other player in major league history to drive in 500 or more runs in his first four seasons. When Albert was told of that distinction, he just raised his shoulders in a shrug.

"I don't compare myself to anybody," he said. "Don't get me wrong, I respect what they did, but it's not my job to make comparisons. I get paid to help my team win."

Helping the Cards win was something that Albert did with great regularity, as he led the league with 34 go-ahead RBI, and 20 outright game-winning RBI, which helped the Cardinals post a 105–57 mark, the best record in baseball, and only one win away from the franchise record that had been set in 1942.

The Cardinals opened the playoffs as

heavy favorites to capture the NL pennant, and they took the first step toward that goal by taking three out of four games against the Los Angeles Dodgers, as Albert went 5–15 with a pair of homers and five RBI. Albert's first home run started a Cards' rout in Game 1, and his second, a 3-run shot, was the game-winner in the Game 4 clincher.

"He wants to be the best player of all-time," said Walt Jocketty. "And he's willing to put in the work to achieve that goal."

But Albert's hitting in the division series was just a warm-up for his heroics in the National League Championship Series (NLCS) against the Astros, when he and Houston center fielder Carlos Beltran combined to put on what might be the greatest hitting display in postseason history.

Beltran, who now plays for the New York Mets, had almost single-handedly demolished Atlanta in their Division Series by going off for four homers and nine RBI, while amassing 10 hits in 22 at-bats. Beltran also attacked the St. Louis pitching staff as if he owned them, as he went 10-for-24, with four homers and five RBI against the Cards, and scored an LCS-record 12 runs. His eight homers in a single postseason tied the mark set by Barry Bonds in 2002, although Beltran did it in just 12 games, whereas Bonds needed 17.

Albert became the first player in big league history to hit 30 or more home runs in each of his first four seasons.

The Cards' high-octane scoring machine led them to home victories in the first two games of the series—despite a homer in each game by Beltran—as Albert thrilled the hometown crowd by hitting a two-run shot in the first inning of Game 1, and the game-winning big fly in the eighth inning of Game 2.

But the Cardinals' Big Red Machine

stalled out in Houston, and the Astros turned the series around by taking three straight games. As the series returned to Busch Stadium, the Cards were on the verge of elimination, and Albert spoke about his 0-for-4 collar in the previous game.

"I can't do it every time," said Albert. "I'm a human being, not a machine. All I can do is try my best. I feel bad that I had an opportunity where I could have put my team on top, but didn't deliver. On the other hand, you have to tip your hat to the other team. Sometimes you just get beat. But tomorrow's a different day, and I'll go out to try my best, again, and we'll see what happens then."

"I don't like to see Albert in the batter's box," said Carlos Beltran. "He's so good; he can hit it out against anyone."

What happened next was that Albert stoked a two-run homer in the opening inning of Game 6, rapped a two-base hit to ignite a two-run rally in his next at bat, and then drew a base-on-balls and scored the winning run in the 12th inning when Jim Edmonds cracked a walk-off dinger.

The Astros, however, seemed to have the Cards on the ropes the following day, as Roger Clemens—the only seven-time Cy Young Award-winner in baseball history—was coasting along with a 2–1 lead, with a runner on third and two out in the sixth inning.

"It's amazing to think that he's gotten better every year," said Jason Isringhausen. "And he doesn't seem to have a ceiling."

Albert, who had only two hits to show for his 14 career at-bats against Clemens, fell behind in the count at 1–2, and the capacity crowd at Busch Stadium seemed to hold their collective breath as Clemens fired a fastball toward the inside corner of the plate. But Albert whipped the barrel of his bat around in the blink of an eye, and lashed a double down the left field line that brought Roger Cedeno home from third, and set off a boisterous standing ovation that seemed to be made up of equal parts of elation and relief. The momentum-swinging hit seemed to break Clemens' attention, and Scott Rolen slammed his next pitch over the left field wall, which gave the Cards a 4–2 lead and all the runs they needed to win the game, and the 2004 National League pennant.

"That last at-bat against Clemens is one of the best I've ever had," said Albert, as his teammates celebrated around him. "I'm going to be dreaming about it for the next couple of weeks.

"This is what you dream about when you're a little boy, going to the World Series," added Albert, who hit .500, with four homers and nine RBI, and was named the MVP of the NLCS. "It doesn't get any better than that."

But even before the celebration ended, Albert was ready to put it behind him.

"We won the pennant, and that's amazing," he said. "But it's not over. We still have the World Series in front of us. We need to keep going."

But the Cardinals' exciting ride ran into a roadblock in the form of the Boston Red Sox, who wrecked their dreams with a four-game sweep. The suddenness of Boston's win, its first World Series victory in 86 years, left the Cardinals' feeling somewhat dazed.

"I knew they were a tough team, and that we would have our hands full," said Albert, dismayed that his team had come so close, but had been stopped a step away from winning the World Series. "But I didn't think any team could take four straight from us."

"It's great to be the MVP, but everybody in this locker room deserves to be the MVP. I'll keep the trophy right here for the rest of my career."

NINE

A Most Valuable Player

After a winter spent working out five days a week, Albert showed up at spring training in 2005 and within a few days looked as if he was in mid-season form.

"Albert could start the season today and hit over .300, because he works so hard in the off-season," said Tony La Russa. "I think he's better than ever, and he still hasn't reached his prime."

For Albert, the main motivating factor for all his effort was to help his team take the step they had stumbled over the previous year.

"I got a taste of the World Series last year," explained Albert. "It didn't turn out the way we wanted it to, but, hopefully, we'll get another whack at it this year. It doesn't come in a package, though. You have to work hard to get there, and that's why I made sure I got myself ready for the season. What I lose today, I can't make up tomorrow. I have to do it today. That's what it's all about."

While Albert had spent the winter gearing himself up for another run at a championship, Walt Jocketty had tried to strengthen the pitching staff by trading for Mark Mulder, and then had gone out and signed shortstop David Eckstein and second baseman Mark Grudzielanek to replace Gold Glove-winner Edgar Renteria and Tony Womack, who had left as free-agents, as had Matt Matheny, the team's Gold Glove catcher.

Albert made sure to welcome the new players and, as another example of his

"He has a lot of pride in how he plays the game," said Cards' coach Jose Oquendo. "When you're that type of person, you continue to get better."

expanding role as a team leader, he also offered help to the younger players, and to anyone else who needed it.

"I try to pass it along, the same way that veteran players helped me when I came up," explained Albert. "Hopefully, in five years, they can do the same for somebody else.

"And it's not just about helping the younger players," continued Albert. "Jimmy might tell me I'm holding my hands too low. If I see something that's out of sync with Scott, I'll tell him. We all pull for each other. That's why we won 105 games last year, and why we've been to the postseason in four of the past five years. Everybody is helping each other."

The Cardinals did another excellent job of pulling together during the 2005 season, overcoming the departure of a pair of Gold

"Albert would give away money before he'd give an at-bat away," said Cards' hitting coach Hal McRae. "He treats each one as something special."

Glove winners, and a spate of injuries, including a season-ending one to Scott Rolen. Despite those hardships the Cards still managed to win 100 games for the second successive season, and once again posted the best record in baseball.

"Albert is the best right-handed hitter in baseball, and with Barry Bonds hurt, he's the best hitter in the game, period," said Astros' catcher Brad Ausmus.

A key element in the Cardinals' success was its pitching staff, which led the majors with a 3.49 earned run average. At the top of the starting rotation was Chris Carpenter, who went 21-5, and earned the National League Cy Young Award, while Mark Mulder did the job he was brought in to do by notching 16 wins. The relievers also played their part, especially Jason Isringhausen, who scored 39 saves and posted a miserly 2.14 earned run average.

But the main man in the Cardinals' ride to their second straight divisional title was, once again, Prince Albert, whose presence and hitting feats stabilized an often-makeshift lineup. His hitting seemed to be as reliable as an atomic clock and as consistent as a metronome. From April through September, he compiled better than a .300 average in every month of the season, except for August, when he came in at .287. Likewise, his on-base percentage was higher than .400 in every month but April, when it was .396.

"There's not a pitch he can't hit," said Tino Martinez. "There aren't any holes in his swing, and he has a game plan for every pitcher he faces."

"We talk about Barry Bonds having been the greatest hitter of our time right now," said Washington Nationals' general manager Jim Bowden. "Get ready for Albert Pujols, because he's next. He's got the potential to be one of the greatest hitters ever to play the game. That's not an exaggeration. That's what he is."

Albert continued his rampage in the postseason, as he led the high-flying Redbirds to a three-game sweep of the San Diego Padres, and into a return match in the LCS against the Astros, a team they had finished 11 games in front of in the regular season. But after the Cardinals won the first game, the Astros took three straight, and held a 4-2 lead with two outs in the top of the ninth inning of Game 5, and Brad Lidge, one of the league's top closers, on the mound.

"I don't take any hitter lightly," said Brad Lidge. "But, when you're facing Albert Pujols, you have to be at the very top of your game."

The fans at Minute Maid Park were on their feet, screaming for Lidge to get the final out and give Houston its first-ever National League pennant. But Eckstein singled and Edmonds drew a walk, which brought Albert to the plate.

Lidge got ahead in the count, 0-1, as

the Houston fan noise grew close to deafening, but then Albert sucked the noise and the life out of the park by cracking a 412-foot drive over the left field fence that gave the Cards a 5-4 lead and sent the series back to St. Louis.

"It was amazing how quickly the silence fell on the crowd," said Albert, who had been 0-4 in the game. "It went from being so loud that I couldn't hear the guys in the on-deck circle, to hearing my own footsteps as I rounded the bases. That's never happened to me before. Hopefully, I'll get more big hits in this series, and then some more in the World Series."

"He's as gifted a hitter as I've seen come along in a very long time," said former manager Sparky Anderson. "Before he's done, we might be saying he's the best of them all."

But Albert's hopes of returning to the World Series were wiped out by a Game 6 loss that earned the underdog Astros a trip to the Fall Classic for the first time in the franchise's forty-four year existence.

Although Albert didn't reach his goal in the postseason, his .330 average, 41 homers, and 117 RBI in the regular season did earn him his first National League MVP Award. Albert beat out a pair of worthy contenders, Andruw Jones and Derrek Lee, both of whom turned in career years. Jones, Atlanta's superb center-fielder, had led the league with 51 dingers and 128 RBI, while winning his eighth consecutive Gold Glove, while Lee, the Chicago Cubs' silky-smooth first baseman led the league with a .335 average, and also topped the charts in most of the other major offensive categories, while pocketing his second successive Gold Glove.

"If you want to be like him, you have to be willing to work like him," said Miguel Cabrera, the young hitting star of the Florida Marlins.

"The amazing thing is that 2005 was just Albert's *average* season," said Lee, who was gracious about his third-place finish in the voting. "This is nothing new for him. Not only does he have the talent, but his consistency is also a testament to his character and his work ethic. He has stayed hungry every single season. And what is he? Twenty-five? Whew! He'll be one of the greatest hitters ever before he's through. He's going to be in the Hall of Fame, simple as that."

TEN

Winning It All

One day after the Cardinals were eliminated from the playoffs by the Astros, Albert, who had hit .329 with runners in scoring position in 2005, and had racked up a league-high 36 go-ahead RBI, called his friend and personal trainer, Chris Mihlfeld, and told him that they needed to get to work on his off-season routine, with a concentration on Albert's situational hitting.

"But that's what Albert is all about," said Mihlfeld. "He's always going to find a reason to be unhappy with his game, because he believes if he doesn't do that, his game will level off. He doesn't want to level off."

Albert's drive and determination to keep raising the level of his game, to become the best possible player he can be, had already allowed him to achieve goals that no other player had ever reached. He had, for example, become the first player ever to hit for at least a .300 average with 30-plus homers, and 100-plus RBI in each of his first five seasons.

"When you're talking about the best five-year start in major league history, that's *huge*," said Tony La Russa. "It's historic, and you don't see history made that often. But the best thing about him is that he isn't interested in piling up empty numbers or seeing himself on the highlights. He's also trying to do whatever it takes to win the game. I've seen him take an 0-4, but late in the game he'll take a walk to start a rally. And that's

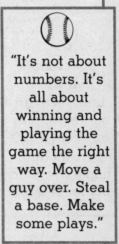

"It's not about numbers. It's all about winning and playing the game the right way. Move a guy over. Steal a base. Make some plays."

what I admire most: He plays the game for the team."

Albert is so focused on winning the next game that he doesn't dwell on what he's already accomplished, although he's constantly asked to do so.

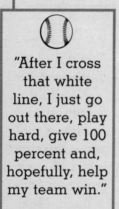

"After I cross that white line, I just go out there, play hard, give 100 percent and, hopefully, help my team win."

"Who really cares about what I did in the past five years?" asked Albert, rhetorically. "That's over with. I'm too young to sit back and think about my past accomplishments. All I want to do is win championships."

Although Albert seems genuinely unconcerned about previous achievements and truly focused on team goals, Cards' hitting coach Hal McRae thinks that Albert has some grand ambitions that he isn't willing to share with anyone else.

"Everyone else can sit back and marvel at what he's already accomplished, but that isn't what he's about," said McRae, a former All-Star outfielder. "Albert has a fire inside of him that always burns hot. He has some goals that he doesn't talk about. Whatever they are, he's still moving toward them."

Albert started the 2006 season as though he was absolutely going to reach whatever goals he might have set for himself, no matter how high he may have set them. He began his roll by becoming the first player to hit a home run in the Cards' initial game at the new Busch Stadium. But that was merely the start of a month-long barrage that saw Albert blast a total of 14 big flies in April, breaking the major league record of 13 that had been shared by Ken Griffey, Jr. and Luis Gonzalez.

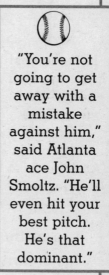

"You're not going to get away with a mistake against him," said Atlanta ace John Smoltz. "He'll even hit your best pitch. He's that dominant."

By the beginning of June, Albert already had 25 homers and 65 RBI, and was on track to break the all-time single-season home run record of 73 that had been set by Barry Bonds in 2001.

"There is no ceiling for this guy," said David Ortiz, the Boston Red Sox' big bopper. "I guarantee you he's going to have a career year. I wouldn't be surprised if he hits 60 or more home runs this year."

"He's the best hitter I've ever seen," said teammate Chris Carpenter. "And the most dangerous."

A few days later, however, Albert suffered an injury that put him on the sideline for 15 games, which sidetracked his run at the record book. But one day after his return to the lineup, Albert was back rocking the ball, and finished the season with career highs in home runs (49) and RBI (137). As usual, Albert came through when the Cards needed him most, slugging a pair of game-winning homers in the final week of the season that carried the slumping Cards to their third straight division title.

"Those were the hugest of the huge," said La Russa. "Albert is the greatest prime-time hitter in baseball, and he proved it again, right when we needed it the most."

Albert continued to deliver big blows in the opening round of the playoffs, as he drove in the game-winning runs in two of the Cards' three wins that allowed them to close out the Padres in the Division Series, 3-1.

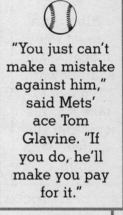

"You just can't make a mistake against him," said Mets' ace Tom Glavine. "If you do, he'll make you pay for it."

"He's a game-changer," acknowledged San Diego outfielder, Brian Giles. "He's a threat every time he's up."

Albert's joy at advancing to the NLCS against the New York Mets was tempered by the news of the death of his uncle Antonio, who had helped to raise him.

"I can't believe he's not here," said Albert. "I still think of him as being alive."

Despite his heavy heart and a strained hamstring, Albert, who hit .318 in the series, still played a key role in the Cards' exciting seven-game win over the Mets, who had tied for the best record in baseball during the regular season with 97 wins.

"Albert is a great role model," said Ryan Howard. "I'd like to take it to his level and stay up there with him."

The Cards, who had won only 83 games during the season, the second-lowest total ever for a pennant-winning team, were decided underdogs to the Detroit Tigers in the World Series. But the Cards turned the tables on the Tigers and the odds-makers, and took four out of five games and captured their first World Series since 1987. Although his bat was quiet during the series, and role-players like David Eckstein, who was named the Series MVP, were the shining stars, no one celebrated more joyously than Albert, who had achieved his grandest goal.

"This is what I dreamed about," said Albert, a smile spread wide across his face. "I finally have a World Series ring, and that's what I play for. I'm going to enjoy this feeling for a few months, and then I'll be ready to go after the next one."

When the regular-season awards were given out a month after the end of the World Series, Albert finished second in the voting for the MVP Award, the runner-up to Philadelphia Phillies' first baseman Ryan Howard, who had led the majors in homers and RBI. Ironically, Albert had had what was probably his best season to-date, as he won his first Gold Glove, and led the NL with a .397 batting average with runners in

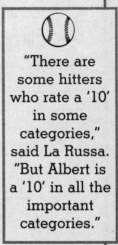

"There are some hitters who rate a '10' in some categories," said La Russa. "But Albert is a '10' in all the important categories."

scoring position, and was the only hitter in the league to finish in the top five in average, homers, RBI, runs, on-base percentage, and slugging percentage.

"Despite the voting results, Albert is the best player in baseball," declared Tony La Russa. "And before he's finished, he'll be recognized as one of the greatest ever to play the game."

ALBERT PUJOLS CAREER STATS

HITTING STATS • REGULAR SEASON

SEASON	TEAM	G	AB	R	H	2B	3B	HR	RBI	TB	BB	SO	SB	CS	OBP	SLG	AVG
2001	St. Louis Cardinals	161	590	112	194	47	4	37	130	360	69	93	1	3	.403	.610	.329
2002	St. Louis Cardinals	157	590	118	185	40	2	34	127	331	72	69	2	4	.394	.561	.314
2003	St. Louis Cardinals	157	591	137	212	51	1	43	124	394	79	65	5	1	.439	.667	.359
2004	St. Louis Cardinals	154	592	133	196	51	2	46	123	389	84	52	5	5	.415	.657	.331
2005	St. Louis Cardinals	161	591	129	195	38	2	41	117	360	97	65	16	2	.430	.609	.330
2006	St. Louis Cardinals	143	535	119	177	33	1	49	137	359	92	50	7	2	.431	.671	.331
	Career Totals	933	3489	748	1159	260	12	250	758	2193	493	394	36	17	.419	.629	.332

HITTING STATS • POST SEASON

SEASON	TEAM	G	AB	R	H	2B	3B	HR	RBI	TB	BB	SO	SB	CS	OBP	SLG	AVG
2001	St. Louis Cardinals	5	18	1	2	0	0	1	2	5	2	2	0	0	.200	.278	.111
2002	St. Louis Cardinals	8	29	5	8	1	1	1	5	14	5	6	0	0	.400	.483	.276
2004	St. Louis Cardinals	15	58	15	24	4	0	6	14	46	8	6	0	0	.493	.793	.414
2005	St. Louis Cardinals	9	32	7	12	2	0	2	8	20	5	3	0	0	.447	.625	.375
2006	St. Louis Cardinals	16	52	11	15	3	0	3	6	27	13	10	0	1	.439	.519	.288
	Career Totals	53	189	39	61	10	1	13	35	112	33	27	0	1	.429	.593	.323

ALL STAR GAME • HITTING

SEASON	TEAM	G	AB	R	H	2B	3B	HR	RBI	TB	BB	SO	SB	CS	OBP	SLG	AVG
2001	St. Louis Cardinals	1	0	0	0	0	0	0	0	0	1	0	0	0	1.000	.000	.000
2003	St. Louis Cardinals	1	3	0	1	0	0	0	1	1	0	0	0	0	.333	.333	.333
2004	St. Louis Cardinals	1	3	1	2	2	0	0	2	4	0	0	0	0	.667	1.333	.667
2005	St. Louis Cardinals	1	2	0	1	0	0	0	0	1	0	0	0	0	.500	.500	.500
2006	St. Louis Cardinals	1	3	0	0	0	0	0	0	0	0	1	0	0	.000	.000	.000
Career Totals		5	11	1	4	2	0	0	3	6	1	1	0	0	.417	.545	.364

FIELDING STATS

SEASON	TEAM	POS	G	GS	INN	TC	PO	A	E	DP	FPCT
2001	St. Louis Cardinals	1B	43	32	287.0	307	283	19	5	27	.984
2001	St. Louis Cardinals	3B	55	52	431.2	161	40	111	10	17	.938
2001	St. Louis Cardinals	OF	78	70	611.2	139	128	6	5	0	.964
2002	St. Louis Cardinals	1B	21	16	144.0	154	140	13	1	24	.994
2002	St. Louis Cardinals	3B	41	37	293.0	97	25	66	6	6	.938
2002	St. Louis Cardinals	SS	1	0	2.0	0	0	0	0	0	.000
2002	St. Louis Cardinals	OF	118	101	873.2	181	173	4	4	0	.978
2003	St. Louis Cardinals	1B	62	36	369.2	374	340	33	1	34	.997
2003	St. Louis Cardinals	OF	113	113	904.1	208	198	7	3	0	.986
2004	St. Louis Cardinals	1B	150	150	1338.2	1582	1458	114	10	136	.994
2005	St. Louis Cardinals	1B	157	154	1358.2	1708	1597	97	14	175	.992
2006	St. Louis Cardinals	1B	143	142	1244.1	1464	1348	110	6	145	.996
Career Totals			982	903	7858.2	6375	5730	580	65	594	.990